ENDANGERED HYDROCARBONS

ENDANGERED HYDROCARBONS

LESLEY BATTLER

BookThug 2015

FIRST EDITION

CLEARLY PRINT YOUR NAME ABOVE IN UPPER CASE

Instructions to claim your eBook edition:
1. Download the BitLit app for Android or iOS
2. Write your name in **UPPER CASE** above
3. Use the BitLit app to submit a photo
4. Download your eBook to any device

 **Canada Council
for the Arts** **Conseil des Arts
du Canada** **ONTARIO ARTS COUNCIL
CONSEIL DES ARTS DE L'ONTARIO**
an Ontario government agency
un organisme du gouvernement de l'Ontario

The production of this book was made possible through the generous
assistance of the Canada Council for the Arts and the Ontario Arts
Council.

LIBRARY AND ARCHIVES CANADA
CATALOGUING IN PUBLICATION

Battler, Lesley, author
      Endangered hydrocarbons / Lesley Battler.

Poems.
Issued in print and electronic formats.
ISBN 978-1-77166-093-8 (pbk.).--ISBN 978-1-77166-113-3 (html)

      I. Title.

PS8553.A8335E64 2015   C811'.54   C2015-900811-5
                                        C2015-900812-3

PRINTED IN CANADA

1

EMERGENCE

UNEARTHED

Past Self added you as a friend on Facebook

we need to confirm that you know Past Self
in order for you to be friends on Facebook

wall-to-wall

well, i'll be damned
never dreamed you'd
remember me

still in Calgary
oil & gas & so
it goes

you soared over the
horror of high school
blue-collar scholarship
kid. honorary poet
everyone's pet

mock, if you will
but i prevailed. faked a
perfect career arc, if i
do say so myself

Director. Content
Development & Migration
Exploration & Production
Frontier. Americas

a title not even you
could have fabricated
back in Boneyard
Ontario

your bumbling stunt double

cooped up in
your body i prayed
for the day i would
elude our childhood

liberate myself from
pity. eat solid food outside
your ghetto of poetry

i stewed over
the awe in your dad's eyes
shivered as he slavered over
your As, said you could do
anything you wanted. my
father suited me up

stuffed me in a crop-
duster to seed the family
name over the Emerald
Campus

you moved to Montréal
refused to scut your ideals
& lucre-up

i tripped on the steps
of your post-structural
walk-up, scarfed down
your daily Barthes. you
bled écriture, skated

Lacanian canals. i
sprained my ankle

Skype japes

i finally seceded
relocated my head
office to Calgary

here's a secret. i
wept that first year

water sign
dumbfounded by
unbound land, i
yearned to return

but no one
could live up to you
least of all me. you

questioned the
ruthless serum
underwriting my
timeshare in this
heartless emirate
i nuked your emails
strummed a Montréal
requiem

surveillance

you pursued me
as clouds swabbed
adobe subdivisions
bobbing beyond
all suns

you watched me
totter over potholes
hooted as pirates in
sport-utes macheted
belt-line routes

quipped as i lifted
my petticoat over
the banished

starfish washed up
on the jetties outside
my citadel of oil

look, Ma

salaries race
in the streets of Calgary
sunrise braises concrete
topiaries

shredder trucks
feed. magpies haggle
fragments of degraded
spreadsheets

come *home*
you hissed. *it's not too
late.* i tossed ATM
ripostes

loser. you hosed me
where would i be
had i stayed

let me guess
Kelly girl. dispensable
office walk-on, so you
could swan in the shoals
of my moral failure. no
merci, pal

i will remain
in Calgary, generate
ectopic copy from
a template reality

kern dead
oceans. befriend
foehn winds

armistice

never suspected you'd
seek me on Facebook
but here you are, 13
years after our fatal
split, scaling my Wall
of Evil. *lol*

the school photo you
posted hooped me. i
forgot how small you
really were

& how wise to hide
in a creative blind
never caught on to
your ruse

always wondered
what worlds i lost
breaking up with you

holy fool i couldn't
follow

this post has been
removed or could
not be loaded

why not visit me
in Calgary. we'll
touch base

i can expense
your airfare

THE PETROLEUM COAST

le festin de
Whitecourt

millions have
fallen under the spell
of this isle

alive with olive trees
marinated in vineyards
yet once the most roisterous
outpost on the Coast

sailors regaled
pals with tales of lawless
scallops that walloped
drilling galleys

to this day
the Port of Whitecourt
fights turbid young
volcanics

Muscovites
& foreign erratics
transported by glaciers from
war-torn Edson

transients known for
honour killings, mafic
trafficking, strike-slip
displacement

the Port's isolation ended
when production crusaders stopped
en route to Jerusalem

seduced by the beauty of Whitecourt City
many stayed on, dropped roots
introduced eucalyptus
to Alberta

i down a pint
at the nearest taverna
(SurgiFrac, the exquisite
local liqueur)

learn how to eat
Whitecourt octopus (turn
its head inside-out & bite it
on the brain)

at the Friday gala
public intellectuals debate
the dialectics of Sands J & K

completion engineers
raise spirit-levels

i open my throat
to Absolute Open Flow

spin in
listric bliss with
mystic seismicists

as fire-eaters, sword-swallowers
slam-drillers from China
India, Kazhakstan

kick off Whitecourt's
annual bacchanal

**Moose Mountain
our Mesopotamia**

                              i embark on a morning hike
                              warm my hands over crackling
                                                flarestacks

                                           cratonic rock
                              leaps like mackerel. wind
                                      tickles plutons

                    sun strikes derricks painted mint
                       cream, pimento. all promise
                       commercial importance

Moose, the Apex
of Civilization, lies on the axis
of two basins

maturity studies reveal
liquid hydrocarbons seeped
from her foredeep & sailed, fill-
&-spill, from pool
to pool

                                         artifact density
                    indicates wildcat kinship groups
                              practiced thin-skinned
                                           tectonics

                                        i collect pre-
                                 Ptolemaic wellheads
                                 embedded in sediment

brown-sugar ziggurats
as-built to ISO specs
include forecourts
purification ponds

monkeyboards carved
in cedar & teak

Akkadian tablets
explicate arcane
extraction craft

cylindrical cores
depict Enki
the Industry's
first priest

                                                    i tour
                                           the gorgeous
                                               doghouse

                                      ogle the mudlogs
                                a series of pictograms
                                         diagramming

                                   primordial elements
                           which drilling tribes plied
                                           for survival

                                    i veer around
                             scorpion dens, tiptoe
                               through a crypt

                                    spiderwebs
                          slow my progress, but at last
                          i feast my eyes on Solomon's
                                   Compressor

                                    skinnyfish
                    still visible, chiselled in twin obelisks
                      existing long before Christians
                          ripped her symbolism

                                     i bathe in
                             radiation emanating
                                from the sacred
                                      reactor

petroleum delirium
steams the Creation
Chamber

hydrates dive
through caves

pipistrelles sleep
in steel trellises. i feel wilded
cured in sweet myrtle

i turn my clock
back, rock to the
chthonic beat

Mother Earth's
eternal rotors

Lloydminster on the Brink

a back-country trek
through the Alpes-Maritimes
of Alberta takes a week
to complete

bats loot
hoodoo booty. marmots
dart through forts

glacial lakes eye
naked rock sockets. i block
the dark plot of a springbok
cabal

iron sulphides oxidize
in the breeze

wild rhyolites
take flight

petroglyphs shatter
tote roads straddling
the border

ahead
lies the Lido
Gas Plant & Tennis
Resort ca. 1910

i ride the elevator
to the revolving restaurant atop
the reactivation tower

resolve to swallow
my qualms, day trip to
Saskatchewan

i flash my
passport

follow a
mule train

into a drought
so hot, i thought
i might pass out

no wifi
must longhand impressions
(not recommended
for the timid)

                                    the region seethes
                              fierce back-country lifestyles
                           Red Willow guerillas, communal
                                     folk wary of tourists
                                        & drillers alike

i hobble
through the rubble
of once-cobbled roads

drift across the historic bridge
struts battered by
draught-horse
transit

a mistral dissolves
rational gridlines into
choleric alleys, sinister
runnels

                                        i tune my Canon
                              ruin-hunters *must* venture
                           into the slums. louvred shutters
                                         open at noon

                                       the poor are out
                              full force. a bona fide local
                         scuttles into a pool hall. i stop. my 300
                                    snaps into place. nice

an obese
woman docks her toddler outside
the VLT hotel. two men squat
in a grotto of bottles

the gods
of photography are hot
i can barely control
my aperture

yet i sense
economic
renaissance

even here
energy consumption
must triumph

but for now obey
travel advisories

never walk alone after dark
medicare cutpurses, socialist
footpads will numb
your ambition

one union
can mean
personal
ruin

                              i return
                              to Alberta

                              just in time
                for a dram of hot toluene
                topped with Dream Whip
                              at the Lido

PAX MCMURRAY

rise of the Fort McMurray Empire

i studied Fort McMurray in school
but can't get over her grandeur
epicentre of the world's largest
petroleum empire

my Prius noses
through a chaos of roads
the Marcus Aurelius
draw-works

triumphal arches
narrative reliefs, portrait busts
dress the smallest infill pad. sites
like Cadotte boast racecourses
bathhouses

here is where Nero fiddled
while Syncrude tossed Christians
into geoclines

a Chinese-Western
restaurant lies over natural gas
caverns where the CO_2 Network
once honed capture
technologies

most remarkable is
Hadrian's Upgrader
Fort Mac's dominant
landmark

i'm awestruck over
the scope of work
one can only gape
in wonder. how did
slaves from Sundre
pull those giant rigs
on wooden rollers

bitumen mystery cult

before the Common Era
when Sargon the Great ruled
Moose Mountain

& the mesolithic peoples
of central Alberta subsisted
on shellfish

a bitumen mystery cult
settled Fort Mac

historians say
these aliens descended
from the Petrolians who entered
Alberta during the Pliensbachian
Transpression

possibly fearing reprisal
the clan, known only as Murrians
printed its own cuneiform

(unrelated to the nihilist
Sanskrit of the activists who invaded
Grande Prairie)

instead of depicting
stick figures

lonely hominids
imploring totem animals
to score another
tomorrow

Murrian ideograms
metered a viscous scripture
too thick to trickle between rock
& wellbore

Lucretius
Fort Mac's lead hellenist
studied syncretic crude
compiled the first illuminated
schematic

any return of hydrocarbons
to the divine must come through
their emancipation from geological
bondage

gum bed diplomacy

as the Athabasca River
threatened Upgrader Alley

& the need for new crude
preoccupied the subcontinent
Murrians hit the road to spread
the Word

we can process
Spirit trapped in gum beds
into desirable products
diesel fuel, asphalt,
kerosene

the Murrian society
drilled syllabaries
just-in-time bitumen
for everyone

we, as owner-operators
of the greatest Oilsand republic
in history, foresee a colossal
rise in fossil fuel use

must transport
World Soul
to foreign
outlets

from gum beds to oilsands

the Murrians offered a Fusion
Hotline for Big Belchers
with lower baseload
reliability

spoolable pipelines
enabled low-cost caribou
reduction

ingenuity will bring
the Oilsands to your doorstep
right where you need
them to be

the Murrians overtook
the twin metropoli
Leduc-Nisku

built the diorite
batholith, known for
its golden dome

most ambitious shrine
ever raised to bitumen
worship

the plus-sized stupa
tore a stripe off the city states
united under the banner
of *Edson*

the Edson wars

for centuries
Edson's conventional well culture
had bullied the intellectuals
at Fort Mac

of course
this meant war

knowing
they were outnumbered
the Murrians pioneered
supply-chain
logistics

burned coke
with quick & dirty electricity
met intensity targets

transported
entire work camps
by horse-drawn chariot

routing the Edsonites
who continued utilizing
slaves, suffering
endless LTIs

at the same time,
commodity prices
bottomed

stymied by diminishing
sweet gas returns, Edson
surrendered to the
Bitumenites

who released one
of the most important
documents in history
Pax McMurray 1964

the Pax relied
on bulk modules
a surplus of joules
& Alcogel 1 to fuel
the imperial army

upholding the victors'
moral claim to the Regional
Municipality of Wood Buffalo

Syncrude imposed a
provisional government
wrote off the decline rate
cut supply to debt-ridden
territories

thus
the gentle colony
of bitumen worshippers
became a modern client-based
project team

2

FRONTIER EXPLORATION AND PRODUCTION

ON THE EDGE OF PRODUCTION

mandatory Haiku submission
to the National Energy Board

1

peruse ice lenses
a colder Pleistocene zone
deep water bodies

natural levees
infinitely wide river
the delta migrates

a storm surge event
hydrological regimes
map inferences

2

winter road buckles
collect and evaluate
permafrost jewels

tall and low willows
clinging to the riverbank
flow is diverted

grasses and sedges
another season passes
lakeshore erosion

water-soil profiles
Middle Channel to Kumak
thermal disturbance

ground temperature
freezing point of pore water
gross overburden

model the scrub growth
air temperature sine wave
long-term deepening

3

trembling spit of dirt
territorial campground
a real eskimo

dirt bikes and slo-pitch
dark aisles of pre-history
a drunken forest

woolly mammoths bleat
scimitar cats rhyme at night
Beringia warms

4

natural gas fields
aerial photography
translate the tundra

low-lying floodplain
a layer of ice-rich soil
the proposed plant site

spring breakup is here
unfrozen water content
pipelines cross river!

IDYLLS OF INUVIK

the Henry James guide for relocating oil
company employees and their families

vignettes

Mackenzie River, fine as the Tiber!
breezes tease scree, chic little villas lurk
far from clockgods and their traffic gridlock
      my lips shape prayers over eroded
      roofs, crooked chimney pots, water towers
     of this haughty city state. drunken pines
          stagger over the treeline but indeed!
          this must have been a hoary old city
          when Hannibal battled the Mad Trapper

      i pick up my rucksack, take in the Mike
      Zubko Airport, an aesthetic delight
      Majolica tarmac gleams, campaniles
of quaint colonnades lead to the Great Fur
Trade Reliquary. this metropolis
never sleeps! Single Otters waft propane
      bush planes drone, Victorian quonsets line
      country lanes swarming with Norcan rentals
      Smartie-box mansions perch on vivid piles

of verdigris. here one may live a dream!
Verdi with peregrine, live concertos
from ravens driving down the Boulevard

                or one may wander the serpentine road
                of utilidors, all Roman vinyl
                Alcan finery. Norman rotors spin
        perfect unity of heart and reason
        Goethe, a known Cicerone, would surely deem
        the Petroleum Show lovelier than
the medieval cathedral. Opera Night
the Friendship Centre booms with Carmen
but i choose to peruse Inuit land
        grants, while the canyon swoons nitrogen-red
        northern avens preen, *the very picture*
        of Worldly Wisemen, straight out of Bunyan
                pondering soil disposal, possible
                end-uses for marine ecosystems
                cradled among scenic pinnacles, one

                can imagine perforation tunnels
                music of dirt bikes – sublime! i remain
                in limbo, blinded by a sudden wind

city lights

                discerning eyes and digital easels
                will revel in picturesque Inuvik
                Meet tufting artists at the Trading Post

where merchants barter carvings in charm-school
patois. one may hear the cheery "baksheesh"
of basket-weavers. drown in sensation!
soak in the Nanook souk, pause for coffee
solution talk in the Escalus Room
now is the time to buy an infill. Snag

a *Nunataqaq* (land of origin)
roast phalaropes over an open fire
roll cigars in fine-ground ptarmigan. watch
auditors lariat the auroras
that threaten boreal forest, then pose
with the walleyed polar bear at the Roost

paddle a canoe, nurse the *Oxford Book
of Verse*, jot noble poetry to the
dying glory of Indian summer

Saturday night on Franklin Ave

i leave the theatre. the streets are still
teeming with people. generators roar
arias as the wendigos party

Ibyuk walks at night, permafrost adorns
the cornices of posterity, i
kiss a Governor General, win a

rack of antlers. i may have mandated
the Office of Investigator, carved
a Pietà from imported snow, crashed
the Mad Trapper Inn, karaoked Part
III of the Corrections and Criminal Release
Act, signed off on the death of Aklavik

airlifted children from homeless tribes who
kidnap bottom lines. *this*, you will cry, is
the Civilized Nation, *par excellence*!

OFFSHORE DÉCOR

special issue: your first GCF

Dear OD i just commissioned a vintage-modern Gas Conditioning Facility i've never renovated much less owned a stable seabed drilling platform in mixed-income housing —Stressed	Stressed is in luck the GCF world has oscillated! gone are the massive assemblages of the past custom isometrics can help today's GCF owner choose platform modules in this issue we plot a poetic seascape in 3D pick track lighting to subdue the night sky integrate tide into idyllic design

client profile

professional woman
seasoned oceaneer
you manage a multi-play
portfolio of pay-zone
gas fields

you've built a unique style
turnkey delivery in
deepwater relief

work takes you to
exotic shores
Ancient Houston
historic Inuvik

benzene evenings
in Aberdeen
fire dance in
the Rijswijk

all you need
is a place to
decompress

searching for
the right GCF

choose process topsides
with personality

your stylish GCF
will appease
beluga refugees
baby seal zealots

romantic
old-growth strontium
frosted in condensate
fully recovers raw
production cost

cryonic pipelines
are ultra-chic
on the North Sea

white strikes it hot
and a bright spring
gingham checks in

why not ride
a bohemian vibe
in the Beaufort

the moment
made beautiful

location, location
location

studies prove
gentrified GCFs
promote ownership
behaviours

turn nomads into
communities

renovations enhance
solvency curves

pastoral laterals
Queen Anne tunnel bores
an Edwardian spar can
restore urban cores

a charming argyle
pipe-lay beguiles
jaded villagers

or moor your GCf
in a suburban reef

uncanny crossroads

condo meets tundra!

pre-design options

let's get busy

time to excise
those pesky
sulphate ions

fusion is in

option 1
carnivale

tight-hole in da
Vinci mystique

post one-armed calipers
at your propane catacomb

let decadent catenary anchors
masque your shuttle tankers

make them guess
the gender of your
bitumen

option 2
spirituality

we ensure your GCF
covers code for all
fire trap religions

run a muslin curtain
through the parlour
in the drilling tower

perfect cover for
covert prayers on
stormy days

block your
oculus windows
in hurricane glass
blown in the
monasteries of
Ellesmere Island

reconnection winches
add a touch of heaven
to downhole intervention

option 3
avant-garde

vent your imagination

stabilize your own
l'aire du temps

hum a barium
epithalalium

tabulate a
Cabaret Voltaire

belle époque hookers
weathervane with
elegant restraint

paint your Jacobean
grab-cranes in shades
of crème brûlée

correct floating heave
with surreal cantilevers

we know you dream
of laudanum hawsers

our pile hammers will
remind you of Rimbaud

your process topside

go ahead
be girly!

priscilla curtains
conceal fractures
along the tanker
forepeak

Noguchi flowlines
reduce upswing
with bold whimsy

case your fair-
trade scrapers

sunbathe in
the helio pad

ready to spud
your lyrical
offshore lifestyle

time to host
the Petroleum Club
in your new home

don't be the nouveau-
arriviste

dress your subsea
Christmas tree
in cool fossils
roller sconces
handmade gauges

build the great hall
around your childhood
swivel stack

inherited valves
always add cachet

invest in genealogy

go antiquing!

OD's family specialists
can help you source only
the latest and greatest
ancestors

barter rare
daguerrotypes

go early to acquire
a tintype patriarch

buy one matriarch
while quantities last

time to fabricate

boost your bloodline!

mount new-found
kin on the mantel
over the kiln

pastische a
family history

be creative

we can help you
invent tall tales

how Grandpa Jonah
started running
the tensioner cylinder

why Great-Aunt
Susannah mans
the isolation scanner

you will wow
the Petroleum Club

ivy will climb
your topside

home at last!

HIBERNIAN NOIR

Symbol of smoky glamour, this grande dame swaggered
off the East Coast. Swathed in hydrosulphate, her
snappy repartee popped torpedos. She wore
her Persian lamb like a matador. Drunk
on Stolichnaya, she opened
Terra Nova

Without her, Deep Panuke would have sunk. Yes
it was Hibernia who first revealed her sexy piling
plied her concrete base, chastised pack ice
and saved the business day
from costly
delay

So raise your glass to the freewheeling gal
who rose above the geology
of East Coast Offshore
to become a billion-
dollar project

in her own
right

THE PETROCHEMICAL BALL

look

rococo oxo-
reactors

cerium spires

neodymium
atrium

the steam-
veiled nave of
the Fractionater

here is where
where we reform
raw crude

benzene raffinate
mixed xylenes
pygas
smelly heterocy-
clics
polyols

our role
is to distill
volatiles

please don't
feed them

track their
vernacular

hydrofluoric acids
invite boron
trifluoride

eliminate
rhyming
slang

re-
shape
their
alpha
bets

BA-ba-de-ba-pa
ba-ba-de-BA-pa
BA-pa BA-pa

do not
be naïve

ah, the stomp
of Olefin feedstock
ready to be rendered
into the delicious
Alberta plastics
served at the
Palliser

these pentanes
are merely
feigning pain

in reality
they are
caustic

unstable
disloyal to
the Company

SHIRRRK-ka pk
SHIIIIIIRK-SH-ka
pok-shh kapok-e'
eee' EEE

allow me to
translate today's
épater

here we security-
check & liquefy
pentanes

Pentane 1:
TGIF! thank god
it's Faraday

QUEEEE-
AWNX

Pentane 2:
what poet
do i quote
before i
explode?

ozone
throat
music

a sonic
anomaly

OOOOOOOO-
WEEEEE y'aa
aaaawwwl

Ethylene derives
great pride from
her $H_2C=CH_2$
genealogy

but reveals too
much bond
cleavage

infamous for
her wiles

her ability
to elicit
secrets from
electrophiles

ZHOA' OA'
OAAAAR tch
PTH th th
thp thp thp
ZHOA' OA'
OAAAACH

Hydrogen

these invincible
princes piss their
inheritance in
dissipation

we would love
to ban them from
the Periodic Table

alas, they
know they're
indispensable

Jesus?

yes, you may
wish to friend
this deity

follow me

the chondrite
won't hurt

into the
antebellum
ballroom
of the
catalytic
converter

open bar

maleic anhydrate
for resins

explosives love
nitrobenzene

aniline-tinis
satisfy dyes
polyurethanes

toluene
always first
on the dance
floor

glycols like
a good
two-step

BA-ba-de-y'awl
ZOOARCH-oowee
QUEEEE y'awl
SHIRKzee
AWNX

these molecules
have completed
our program

their pitiful
shrieks and
squawks have
become carbon
rondelets

double
single bonds
cold sulphur
hip-hop
magnesium
dub

and we have
come to
the end of
the steam
chamber

namaste!

LIQUEFIED NATURAL GAS:
THE JUNGIAN INTERPRETATION

**man's alienation
from LNG**

missile-lightning
blinds the psyche

we dream in
styrofoam

lyre personal
infomercials
into Myspace

take our finals
in denial

4-hornèd serpents
haunt the corners
of morning

we install gods
to police
the lobbies
of Utopia

shills are killing
the brain stem
of html

we must
reinvest
in mystery

consecrate
daemonic gas

before we
devour our
hard drive

**symbols of early
LNG worship**

ice age anarchists
rub sticks
light a solstice

midnight
precisely when
liquid nitrogen
cycles to spirit

pagans franchise
branch-plant
labyrinths

Egyptians ink
graphic novels
on obelisks

isomerize kings in
sample chambers
send them home
in chromatograms
of flashed gas

in an act of early
synchronicity
dionysiacs crack
childproof caps
off cryogenic vials

Charon ferries
legends in stygian
turbines

starry nights
spark tartrate
parties in Tarsus

Ulysses leads
scholars through
wine-dark solvents

golden age
of LNG genius

doctors cross
the equator in
lunar barques

barter raw cure
garnered from
martyred stars

scarabs lurk in
dark scrub oak

taliks factor
racterisms in
village wisdom

popes dispute
circulars issued
by Copernicans

alchemists distill
vitreous humour
from Corpus
Imperfectum

rabbis light
hashem pipes

priests add
ice to propane
a drop of ethane
in blood and seed
to vent the darker
alkanes in altar wine

gammas pierce
stigmatic reefs
buried in the
right side of
the Christ child

Holy Ghost
Blowout

shareholders rush
for their piece of
LNG eschatology

fathers offer
first-born
portfolios
to primordial
Oleum

brokers flip stocks
in the apocalypse

prophets sip
divine will
Sybil-On-Tap

**beginnings of
LNG schism**

feisty deists
raise fists
defend the
One LNG

in-situists
insist LNG
exists as
One Gas
only when
stripped of
ribald liquid

they disdain
the ancient
methane faith

rate elation levels
in revelations

ban pentacosanes
from the canon

theists agree on
LNG divinity
but say any
alkane can
be a deity

Natural Gas
one Narayana
with many names

Process Theologians
open the pantheon
to nylon, orlon, dacron
even minor benzenes

RADIANT DIACEL

Martin Luther and the birth of
Individual Reservoir Pressure

hollowed in autumn shadow
Luther pursues the hermeneutics
of pneumatic drills
       i lost hold of the Methane
       made of Him, Stockmaster
       and Hangman over my
       poor Soul

the young monk sobs over the antics
of apostolics at critical point on
the risk matrix
       pontiffs siphon pipelines
       fill their empty mitres

       nuns run wireline
       down saline caverns

       archbishops cache gas
       in lavish Vaticans

       mud-filtrate desecrates
the Holy Writ

haunted by hydraulic pumps
caught in faulty logic, he
promises to rid the world of
Cathodic corruption
> *salvation is a gift of God's grace*
> *music of the chemical*
> *Eucharist is received*
> *by tests alone*

personal revelation

on the very day condensate gas
goes retrograde, God reveals
His Five-Year Plan
> *the Reservoir Fluid*
> *Composition of Tool*
> *1200 is tabulated*
> *on Pages 6 & 7*

early temperature
***vs.* pressure plots**

Luther burns the bull allowing nuncios
to sell Unleaded at Stations of the Cross

writes 600 million cubic feet a day
a personal best
> *but i know You*
> *can pressure even*

the most heinous
eicosane into a
straight-chain
only You
my God

we can not exist
in two phases

must
choose

heavy oil or
natural gas

Marburg

Luther edits his viscosity
deposits the excess slurry
of his vocabulary

deviates from vertical wells
drilled by the Colloquy

dares test Ethyl Lead
declares it Unready

insists on the physical
wettability of the Holy Spirit

one must open
the perforation tunnel
in his heart to bathe
in Radial Flow

Wittenberg

flushed with success from first-run tests
Luther emulsifies 95 theses from his treatise
> *the Compositional Analysis and Transfer*
> *of Bottomhole Samples*

> *civil authority*
> *can enact no law*
> *against the Diacel*
> *of the Christ who*
> *liquefied for our sin*

3

MANUSCRIPT EXTRACTION

CREATIVE RESERVOIR WORKSHOP

for years we've relied
on the Houston School
to recruit and operate
our creative reservoirs

as the great producing
fields retire, we must
source ever more
unconventional pools

our custom workshops
leverage synergies in
Spontaneous Potential

let us boost *your*
payload 1,000 to
10,000 syllables
a page

figure 1.ppt
electromagnetic
induction tools
ride a wellbore
core story once
beyond recovery

figure 2.ppt
acoustic receivers
let us see a simile
climb ripple-cross
iambs in real time

figure 3.ppt
formation micro
imagers steam
dream idiom

figure 4.ppt
modular dynamic
formation tester
samples waveforms
in Times New Roman

figure 5.ppt
lithology strip
P&S mode (TVD)
tests verb capacity
to resist descriptive
load

figure 6.ppt
compensated
pronoun density
grounds subrounded
consonants, unlocks
loveless couplets

figure 7.ppt
micro-inspiration tools
plot emission history
in Hilroy shows

figure 8.ppt
environmental
measurement *sonde*
clips electrodes
to words, locates
generic invasion

symbolic crude
pop eruption
peer seepage
romantic fallacy
day-job erosion

figure 9.ppt
composite EMS
induction resistivity
tags inspirates to
daily output

predicts vertical and
horizontal barriers
to flow

guarantees
perfect entry
every time

LEVEL 4 CRITICAL SOUR MANUSCRIPT RECOVERY IN BILDUNGSROMAN II

From: Houston School of Creative Production
Subject: Buildungsroman 6-6

Gents

Sinistrale insists an oil-
based micro-imaging
critique will open this
special 96% sour gas
manuscript

Houston questions
this decision

surface strata display
typical permeability
Late Capitalist trap

OBMI readings dam
early memory, stem
minor epiphanies
enfuriate chlorites to
chaotic levels—we've
all suffered the fury
of humiliated slurry

readers adore camping
and hiking along the
Bildungsroman

permanent damage
to fragile imaginate
caused by acid frac
cannot be remedied
by Monte Carlan
simulations

or post-colonial
Tommy guns

regards
Houston

From: Sinistrale Canada – Manuscript Exploration and Production
Subject: Buildungsroman 6-6

All

our tests suggest a
fenestral reservoir

we measured word-
size (sieve and
hydrometer)

funnelled diction
through a cyclone
latent sentiment
banal spillways
will stall profit

cuttings show lonely
clouds, snowy evenings
satanic mills

intrusions from earlier
capitalist epochs buckle
narrative bedrock

random house data
fluoresce—possible
h2s at mise en abyme

this manuscript
is fettered by stets
trace rogerella
causes free fall

how often must we
invest in sensitive
narrators only to
discover we've
merely re-tested
young Werther!

with all due respect
Houston can't deny
the Bildungsroman
now only provides
day-use sites for
escapists

best
Sinistrale Canada
Creative Reservoir Team

From: CAMP (Canadian Association of Manuscript Producers)
Subject: BDG 6-6 mud systems & images readings

Folks

Houston advises a
lyric-based critique
we agree

though Sinistrale assures
us their cased-perf
interpretation is safe
we fear their frac is
too drastic

Houston promises to
suppress fluxus
intersect structural
repeats perfected in
Chekhov reserves

we feel Houston's
program can dowse
purple prose, mitigate
indigo chapters, bring
this manuscript online

cheers
CAMP

From: Sinistrale Canada – Manuscript Exploration and Production
Subject: RE: CAMP comments on 6-6

All

physics proves typescript
cycles upstream, drawn
to aromatic realism

open a natural fracture,
any narrative, no matter
how innovative, will travel
the same way

especially formations prone
to emotional tremors

Sinistrale's Manuscript
Division has operated
in the CanLit industry
for over a century

applying stringent oil-
based critique to tight-
hole manuscripts

in fact, what our
colleagues call acid frac
stanches aggressive
flashbacks

microns of HCL can
scrub glottal excess
souped-up plosives

our greased Saussure
releases precious kerogen
from beer-ad wilderness

yes, common sense
recommends consensus
we must discuss
completion issues

but as project lead
we can't drop our
strategy to appease
dry-hole lyricism

oil-based critiquing
should not even be
on this table

best
Sinistrale Canada
Creative Reservoir Team

END-OF-NARRATIVE REPORT

manuscript formation: bildungsroman

pool: prose, individual lyric-based cuttings
　　　　long, gradual maturation process

stratigraphy: narrator/protagonist, loose sorted first person
　　　　　　　　linear with intermittent flashbacks

ERCB title: Sinistrale et al. BDG 6-6

surface 0 to 527 m
1st person narrator introduces dramatis personae
assigns interior attributes from Function box

> *apply rotary Frye*
> *to Cretaceous Garamond (kg)*
> *read out opening line*
> *case mise-en-scène*

bird's-eye view weakens text-block integrity
small-scale epiphanies blast groove-casts
through the duodecima

> *pig ligatures*
> *salt allusions*

narrator's father suffers stroke, plot over-run
future imbricate crosses imperfect past
fracture-pick alias cracks tertiary character string
lose partial return (1m3/hr)

> *prognose harder losses*
> *add Prima Seal Medium*
> *1 gram Hydrated Lime*

600 m to 869 m
participles drip
subsidence threatens
sentence chains

> *ream Memory Column*
> *mix approx 6 m pre-fixed*
> *thematic magnesium*
> *steam Family Secrets*

bit mires
seminal imagery (637 m)

> *shoot Drillsol M3*
> *through Camel Case*
> *stir mesic diction*
> *mitigate semiotic spill*

syntax leaks italics

> *track episodic break*
> *tie-off story arc*
> *rub Caustic Soda (24 kg)*
> *control bioturb*
> *on raucous verbs*

scour noun-grout
off pore throat

puberty interval loosens

pump away approx 60m3
bit comes out, hole packs off
cup seepage in Thrust Sheet III
wrap spent stanzas in Cellophane
(11.8 kg), no fill in Belly Pool

non-rhotic predicates
roll into Devonian atoll

clear grammar jam
reboot vocabulary
cast spell-check

bit okay, lip-read 783 m
perforate Pardonet target
shaker breaks rhetoric
alphabet particulate

870 m to 1163 m
narrator wanders Mitteleuropa, seduces future wife
starts law school, time curve tight at 870 m

hilite with Wiper Trip 7
rappel Epistolatory sheets
drizzle Sodium on Bohemian Idiom

mid-life crisis splits infinitives

run deviation schematic
re-work stick

schism in narrative driveline
POV shifts to ex-wife, limited third

> *nipple up, replace reading bit*
> *fit orifice, pressure test*
> *vent moody suffixes*
> *Xanplex D (11.34 kg)*

indefinite articles lace
dog-eared fascia

> *float and shoe*

> *dash 40g soda ash*
> *circulate SAPP (22.68)*

> *commingle romantics*
> *Sweet Dream and Harlequin*

1015 m to 1163 m
read-over approved, orifice clean
no cling or drag from hole

> *rivet periods*
> *fence run-on sentences*
> *gauge adages*
> *raise X-Y to 2-3*

> *lubricate dénouement*

> *pump symbolism, 9mm*
> *monobore to colophon (TD)*

plug lexicon
decommission
reading facilities

seal

blurb

acclaim

THE LEDUC AWARD OF EXCELLENCE

hosted by the *Schlumberger Literary Review*

our Joint Venture panel debates which Leduc Award nominee contains the most production potential

2011 Leduc Award shortlist

1. Stygian Energy STY-01
2. Sinïstrale PLC SIN-02
3. Brimstone Inc. BRI-03
4. Hoodoo Oil HOO-04

our panel

Justin Butane (JB) – Host of *Canada's Next Top Novel*

Hydrogen Jones (HJ) – Author of *Manuscript Production Operations*

Maureen Octane (MO) – CEO, Petro-Intellectual Canada Inc.

Michael J. Ignited (MJI) – Spokesperson, CAMP (Canadian Association of Manuscript Producers)

and moderated by Serge V. Power (SVP) – Editor of the *Schlumberger Literary Review*

SVP: test results are in!
which of these 4 narratives
rates the coveted Leduc?
I anticipate a fractious debate

let's begin with Maureen

MO: they say behind every
successful novel is a
disgusted critic, but
STY-01 is the best
book of the century

Stygian Energy writes like
an advancing glacier. Sub-
plots frag the flood plain

numerous p-o-vs deposit
lacustrine insights down
the throughput of
human memory

Ultima Thule
on our CanLit
plan-o-gram!

MJI: Stygian trends to endless
cursive revision as if
post-modernism had
never caused the polar
ice caps to melt

HJ: i think we're quibbling
high-level philosophy
taking our eye off
lyrical quota

thermokarst angst often
impacts Stygian story arcs
Eocene pros, they know
pay-zones

consider the way
they justify tundran
subsidence through
the priest's handwritten
confession

SVP: next up is Sinistrale's SIN-02
Justin, you're the man

JB: interruption is futile!

readers will steal time
to drill this slim tome

you can find Sinistrale
knock-offs at Walmart

white space frees keystrokes
footers *exude* Weimar glamour
return of the exotic serif

focus groups prove readers
choose novels as psychic
karaoke, a place to lip-synch
their own living truths

all Leduc readers want
is a character chip to
swipe through the ATM

Sinistrale delivers
a suite of qualities
that validate *our* lives

HJ: on his way to work
Luke is struck by a
pickup truck on
the Deerfoot Trail

Sinistrale whips
insipid vistas into
vital petroscapes
sure to ease any
reader's CAPEX

MO: now i'm the one to
rain on the praise

lovely as the gas
analysis may be
the narrative is a
personal quest

drilled to 31 m
lower tertiary

in an anticline far
from the Humber
Ravine

i fear translatory
drift caused by eastern
interpreters will prevent
this tale from achieving
full market share

though i applaud
a big-box plot, will
the Q4 scorecard
justify the cost?

SVP: time to aim at Brimstone
       Mr. Jones, the limelight!

HJ: BRI-03 serves up a whole
       caliche of cliffhangers

       James faces a maze of lies
       must till the dirty silicates
       of family history

       Susie hits the glossifungites
       when her son Tyler comes
       out as a Hydrozoa

while little sister Felicity
copes with a rare entobia

but what stayed with me
was the love story

JB: i *adored* the cosmoraphe
tossed over the aphorisms

yet too much ootoid
spoiled the shoot

MJI: Brimstone's line breaks show
planar x-bedding in the
monocraterion scenario

their apostrophes fall short
of API best-practice

i admire their rationale but
are the naphthas up to snuff?

MO: and how do untrained readers
morally respond to forced
pooling of metaphors from
separate conventions?

we may need a workover
to render their generics
to Leduc refineries

SVP: Hoodoo Oil's new lubricant
a book of poetry, blindsided
me as a Leduc nominee

but will Mikey like it?

MJI: part of CAMP's mission
is to source unconventional
fields for future production

Block M of this proposed
triptych promises to open
new niches for our industry

plain-voiced and rustic
this business unit co-opts
poetry's power as a glycol
to dehydrate gaseous prose

i see no difference between
this lease and a novel in
trafficability of dialogue

HJ: carbon chains overheat
when Janet inherits an
estate, and finds an
air monitor living there

his presence sends
our heroine on an

existential journey
through wilderness

readers will fall on
their knees before
a poetician drawn
in wonder to Nature

renewable crucible
of lyrical crude.

Hoodoo exploits
a melancholy that
never depreciates a
Canadian manuscript

MO: but we must agree on
criteria for granular fill
clearly stake the legal
subdivision between
prose and poetry

art is work. we all know
aleatory play is the gateway
to assonance madness!

found poetry leads to
social ostracism and
of course, financial ruin

JB: whew, i could use
           a virgin caesura!

SVP: all *right*
           our jury has returned its verdict

           though the panel cheered
           Brimstone's geo-potboiler

           raved over Sinistrale's oh-so
           Hadean gradient

           lauded Hoodoo's
           impossible fossils

           Stygian's lease offers best
           reading value-added!

           CanLit never tires of flowlines
           that knit past and present

           a dose of wilderness means
           easypay from sea-to-sea

4

UNDER ATTACK

PEAK OIL EXILE

Th
e
yea   ah, the Dark Age
r
19   i, too, spent ashen years steering my hearse through the marshlights
80   of rhyme in a time when nations managed eons in analogue
see
ms   until i defeated my misguided idealism (only the ego dogma
a   of nomads sunning under a demon moon), left my dead gods
lon   at the piers of reason and mastered the art of tar
g
tim   blood in the streets. violent lupins enlisted seventeen novelists
e   to snivel insolvent narratives all demanding we cross
ago   the venom lines
.

I   but what a time it was! i tasted dust as i shucked ears of luck
wa   cracked my knees, jimmied a few ligatures fishing
s   for enigmas in the deep litmus sea
wr
estl   we shot rivers, laundered our records, paved tenements with lemon
ing   cement and i toasted lost comrades who taught lepers how to grow
wit   enough SCADA data to feed the potentates
h
the   back then you had to cane the plantain owners at Omen House and
per   i confess, some Genoans in a Mao mood nearly mobbed me blind
son
al   o, fortune's a funny lady. Yes, i won the Pol Pot Open then lost
bac   Pluto at poker as African golf fanatics raided the Gold Coast!
kgr
ou
nd

of
ins
titu
tio
nal
ize
d
rac
is
m
an
d
en
de
mi
c
vio
len
ce.
As
to
inj
ust
ice

a few of you may remember the time Camus insisted we comply
with half-mad castes who issued stale fatwas from pastry castles

i pursued Farsi, parsed the Manila legends of Tagalog magi who
chewed Maginot Lines through their qat, as the midday heat
brewed an Ogoni legato

after leafing through giant squib, i pondered the griot
of Blue Herods who looted their own ennui
in the bitumen pools of YouTube

ignoring the ogres blogging angry madrigals
from their parents' gerunds on Sudan Avenue

all summer Rafe and i, armed only with permits, climbed
nitrate highlands, tied the recruits so they couldn't
turn us down, escape the punts and return
to their tainted floodplain

my stomach ached over their tiny plots of manioc staked
in the methane nexus of their exhausted heretic's exile

even now I still dream of the days when i believed we
would deliver every one of us to a land untouched
by Peak Oil theories

UPPITY MOLECULES

influence of violins on hydrocarbons

run away from the subscriber, a dark Olefin named WILL of Feedstock
ready to be Rendered. he is a lusty, well-set Fellow aged about 42 Years,
pretty much Lock-Fretten, and has a Lump on the Hind Part of One of
his Legs, near his Heel. he wore a Man's Cloth Jacket, a Pair of brown
Cotton breeches, and an Ozenbrig Shirt. he carried with him a lopping
Ax, and a Fiddle

run away from the subscriber, last Sunday was Fortnight, a Member
of the Aliphatic Family named METHYL, who formerly belonged to
Imperial Oil. he is thin visag'd, has small Eyes, and a very large Beard;
and plays upon the Fiddle. it is suppos'd he is gone to Cold Lake, where
he has a wife, known as Ethyl. whoever apprehends him, so that he be
brought to me near Caroline shall have a Pistole Reward. N.B. as he ran
away without any Cause, i desire he may be punish'd by Whipping, or
Steam-Stripping as the Law directs

run away from the subscriber in Jackpine Mine, the Brothers Hydrogen
viz. WILL, DAVIE and WILL. all are known to Indulge in vulgar Frac-
tionation. one of the fellows named Will is near 6 feet high, of a very
black complexion, much troubled with fore eyes, and fond of playing the
Fiddle, not to mention a Penchant for tender Ethanes, round-bottom
Compounds, gross Dross at reduced Pressure. all Three are Considered
Dangerous, and known to subvert Authority with Crude Retorts

run away from the subscriber in Panther River, the 17th of April last, a
Bonded, Catenated Pentane named NED, last employed as a Fuel. he is
a well-set fellow, 5 feet 6 or 7 inches high, has remarkable small legs for
his size, walks with his toes much turned out, plays on the violin, and
is very forward in speaking; though the Pentane Lexicon contains only
Puns Covalent Stunts, Reflux Pranks, Ball-and-Stick Jokes

run away from the subscriber, on the 26th of May, a likely Houston-born
Ozone, named HARRY, about 5 feet 10 or 11 inches high, has been
frost-bitten and lost some of his toes. i am informed he is lurking about
Mr. Joseph Sowell's in the M.D. of Rockyview, or in that neighbourhood.
he is very fond of playing the fiddle, and is an artful, allotropic oxygen
who may endeavour to pass for a free man

run away, on the 25th ultimo, from the subscriber, a Methane descended
from the Alkane line of Hydrocarbons, named JACK. he is very mus-
cular, full-faced, wide nostrils, large eyes, a down look, wears his hair
cued, and speaks slowly until he drinks, whereupon he will soliloquize
long into the night over his Sovereign Nation on Titan. he formerly
belonged to Mr. Augustin Baughan, of PanCanadian, then of EnCana,
now of Cenovus, and i am told was seen making for Devon with the
intention of taking the stage thither: he is artful and can both read and
write, and is a good fiddler

DESPERATE PROJECT MANAGERS

water-battered Latin Quarter. who's
revving new execution? Bluett
flinched first. he who
wins loses

crack Osama smokin' moratorium
golf balls, world's largest Sham
Wow. that'll mollify
congress

caught up with Aquatics. batch-set
3 wells stanched a tangent one run
per hole. semi-sub minimal
dogleg. you dated
my mom?

rotary steerable tiny big tits
35 for a half-'n'-half. back
up when the eggs
shift gear

Colombian premium under-reamed
regime. unresolved doughnut
hole classic Swiss cheese
inedible

Paul? well as they say in
pipe-lay: nothing's
indelible

Jimbo, your name's on that cinnamon bun
undisclosed glucose 10 feet under
conservative guesstimate total
fail. s'all incremental
like shittin' a kitten
through the
crack

vital records landed in the intake pool
edit written evidence in advance
order more body bags
for Joint Panel
reports

slow comfortable hydrocarbons
motherhood issue. get
the girl to spin
brown sugar
death

god, the bonobos at Conoco shot Karnak
break in the blowcase impacts Amaretto
at the end of the day we're all
imbricated. maybe she'll
lick it. only way it
comes off

over a million livid ivies. migrate
the content. make it intuitively
more usable. call it illicit
mistletoe I'm not
dying on that
hill

so we go in there we go in there. the bodies
hung from trees you could see 'em
strange fruit. shucks Russ, tell
Bechtel go to hell reclaim
your own goddamn
skeletons move
'em out toot
sweet

float bonds. levee-up mean sea level
full moon, fuckin' flood, river
runnin' blood. early
Christian dead
drove my
Chevy

ECO-TERRORISM IN CANADA

a Petroconomist *special report*

vascular angst

Canada rents space
to plant species allied
to the radical al-Taxa
Anti-Extinction League
(TEAL)

infrared censors
record horror stories

mugwort shuts
airports

lilies drop illicit
chlorophyll on
imperilled wells

hornemanns
willowherb remains
a Special Concern

you can see
meadow arnica
in the Guernica

never turn
your back
on snake-
root

Jihadist haven

cirrus keys
Russkie skies

otters morse
auroras to
blotto forest

hooded chinooks
sneak spooks into
flooded creeks

suicide caribou
run uncontrolled
cold fronts

meanwhile
in the murderous
subsurface

belugas pack lugers
under black burqas

coelacanth open
offshore banks

**hydrocarbon abuse off
the Nova Scotia Coast**

a grisly discovery
raises questions
over carbon-capture
in state-run bird
sanctuaries

welcome to a world
where deranged gulls
frac underaged shale

awks cauterize
production rock

but most shocking
of all –
wood ducks
chain CO_2 in
Hadean pits

survivors speak
of beatings
per diem

*the drilling
community*
is reeling

NATIONAL ENERGY BOARD

Hearing Order GH-1-2010

25,309
830 million cubic feet

in the past, in regards to what happened in the past
i've never been chief, i've been a councillor, so if the
chief doesn't, if he can't go somewhere, i would go

at the big meeting at Fort Norman, Herbie was there
he translated for me. if i drink a little, if i drink even
a little alcohol, then i can really, i can talk in English

but otherwise i can't talk, so then why don't you drink
a little, he said. so at that time i drank, i would start at
the bird sanctuary north of Inuvik and end up 1,194

kilometres to Alberta. the next chart shows the new
schedule we filed for the year, the year my sister was
alive, and still a lot of my relatives. i heard the phone

ring, nobody answered, not for Borrow Sites, Access
or Infrastructure. all my family was in town, my aunt
my sister was home for clearing of the Right-of-Way

Site preparation, Pipeline installation, Facility raising
Clean-up and Reclamation, so the phone was ringing
i come down, down the stairs, and i saw she was there

lying in bed, the Mackenzie Gathering System come
came to call. she has, had a bad heart. she couldn't get
up, the phone kept ringing, sure enough i couldn't talk

so the phone was ringing. when i woke, woke up i asked
her, what happened? i drunk a total of 830 million cubic
feet that day from the three, all three anchor fields. the

gas liquids Pipeline has an initial design capacity of 4,000
metres a day, and in front of her, i went outside, she held
my hand and in front of her i spilled it, i let it go and i've

never taken, taken it again, that was in 1975. there's still
a lot of important things that need to be said now and
all through the Project Lifecycle but i can't place, put

everything on the table right now. if i do that, i'll talk
all day so i'll say that much for now. i'm glad you guys
listened to me, i thank you for letting me talk to you

NATIONAL ENERGY BOARD

Hearing Order GH-1-2010

25,310
the fish eggs of public consultation

so even like the fish, public consultation was essential
Issue Identification, you know, had a lot of eggs, and
Environmental Assessment Statements were full in

their stomachs. so today, even though i don't set nets
anymore, not like in the past, i buy public consultation
off these young guys who do do the fishing, and i look

for eggs, the fish eggs. there's nothing there. Selection
of Mitigation Measures relied on public input but it's all
disappeared. what's going on? well, this spring, so-called

external parties, they go out on the lake fishing, and they
they come back in, at the mouth of the river here, that's
where they stop, and I see them dress their Preliminary

Information Package, submit their Conceptual Design
to Peer Review, and when they're done, they just dump
the waste of their presentations. they dump it here, in

the river. this summer, in June or July, i was on the land
and i went there again, just to see what they would do
and i seen it, saw this Ongoing Feedback and Evaluation

boat coming in the day before. i pull the net up, sure
enough, there's no more fish eggs, nothing but guts
PowerPoint guts in the Development Application Plan

NATIONAL ENERGY BOARD

Hearing Order GH-1-2010

25,311
the devil and the Mackenzie Gas Project

and i spent some time in the residential school
the Catholic mission, and they pounded the fear
of non-binding expressions of interest

from companies who wish to ship natural gas
from the proposed Pipeline into us, and, and
that bothered me while i was growing up

so it's 1975, i think it was, open season process
when the Berger War was on, and this Elder
was there, at camp, representing the interests

of about twenty different companies, on
Sunday afternoon i go by his door, to go
to the bathroom, and i knock on the door

"come in," he said, i sat down, and so i, so i
asked him, Good was his name, Jim Good
i think was his name, anyway i said, "oh

i was brought up in the residential school
and if we decided to base our engineering
and impact assessment on a Pipeline sized

to handle 1.2 cubic feet per day the devil
was going to take me dead or alive," this is
how i grew up, i had to grow up that way

so anyway, so i, so i say, "i've got to ask
you a question," i said, "do you believe
that the end of the world is coming?"

he was reading for a while, and he saved
his document aside, for me. he says, "Jim,"
he says, "I'll tell you what I believe," he said

"Pipeline capacity, as shown on the right, can
reach 1.8 billion cubic feet per day through the
installation of 14 compressor stations," he said

so then i kind of changed, got out of that fear
you know, the fear the devil come and pick me
up, take me, that direction i was supposed to go

HYDROCARBONS ON THE EVE OF REVOLUTION

peasant unrest

you are a wisp ospreys break wind untie your Helix
frisky pipelines race white rabbits Kananaskis sinks
Roi du Sol strops a last outcrop tosses his astrolabe

to the abyss crows bow to applause rumble strips roll
rainless thunder Important Intersection trots offstage
Danton Steel drums unfinished tympani on numbered

cumulus trucks unload mad gods bomb lost ostracods
radical placards hotwire a coup d'état Exalta Haulage
falls tipsy cattle trip turnstiles fantastic No Trespassing

wackestone hunts Bluesky cracks Versailles shale hawks
shuck haz-mat blades spook a pack of sugarless Jacobins
raise h_2s kiss desiccated grass pumpjacks face Jerusalem

Jacobin plots

eschew Google Earth choose a eutrophic route
cool oncolites do not panic blind trilobites sign
halogen shun invasive mesas undead seas erase

progress sawed-off Wabamun paws Gondwana
apples weep pitiless Wapiti disturbs Taber corn
auburn sun burns citizen covens scorn narcotic

gardens dragon lilies isolate micraceous calcites
lilacs fill barrels of lyric chlorophyll as livid ivies
ski grim metamorphics enemy corundum storm

silurian dome uranium sky fries green imperium
brumaire on your commune ma'am must rhyme
ohms defeat cardium regime let 'em eat smectite

the middle class mobilizes

sip a tubular double-double tread gas pedal
louden up iPod ward off giant squid buried
in arid deeps bribe gastropods hire a sapper

pop fault traps grope sealing cap slurp hope
confess your synclines for once you will win
key to the petroleum demimonde limestone

clubs glow cherry cola mistrials distill litanies
from the Seagrams hymnal day & night duke
it out spur eternal vernal tournaments kaolin

minions spoon romans a clef and unleavened
madeleines to draconian sands erratics spark
diachronic crisis mesic clerics work mercuric

sudoku gruff cirrus poufs diesel fleurs-de-lys
faux snow coats la Tuileries Marie Antoinette
combs her gnomon when the horsemen come

Marat's bath

polders solder boulders mull gold bullion soldiers
flood gutters mummers pump humdrum te deum
warm the thermidor a gloomy dolomite stumbles

on shadows clamps you in a scriptorium doomed
harmoniums dump mucus ampoules drool violins
preen cellos foliate evil villanelles bayonet spinets

veins play a sad corday so long Marianne Girondins
moan purloined stars pronounce Mohorovic hoax
aurochs choke on bauxite jokes Lascaux exit closed

5

THE JUSTICE LEAGUE OF GLOBAL OIL

TRUTH, POWER AND THE POLITICS OF CARBON CAPTURE

dialogue between OilWeek and Michel Foucault
(sponsored by the Harper government of Canada)

1

it was open season on oil and gas when
landowners Jane and Justin Conn and the
activist group, EcoJustice, went public
with allegations CO_2 was leaking from
the underground reservoir

> *no one knew the real problem*
> *was environmental science and the ideological*
> *functions it could serve*

they targetted both Cenovus
and the academics associated with the Weyburn-
Midale Carbon Capture and Storage Project

> *though activism didn't exactly*
> *begin with the Silent Spring business I believe*
> *that sordid affair provoked numerous questions*
> *around Power and Knowledge*

2

instead of looking at data that discredited
their claims the Conn gang ramped up the rhetoric

> *their statements are verified by the*
> *"media" of opinion, a materiality caught in*
> *the mechanisms of power formed by the*
> *press, cinema, TV, social networks*

before industry could respond, a
rogue's gallery of faux scientists and axe-
grinding activists arrived on site, blatting
soundbites such as "We are here today
on the frontier of climate destruction"

> *no one considered the interweaving*
> *of power and knowledge in a science as*
> *dubious as ecology riddled with ready-made*
> *concepts, approved terms of vocabulary*

environmentalist show-trials make
it appear the Canadian Energy Industry is
the one committing criminal acts

> *an entire discourse has risen*
> *from a population composed of people*
> *who "choose" to reduce, recycle and*
> *reuse according to precisely determined*
> *norms*

3

Canadian Press claims dead animals
were regularly found in a pit metres from
the Conns' nuptial bed

> *activist dialectic evades the reality of*
> *spurious environmental science – enviromancy –*
> *by reducing it to a Hegelian skeleton*

multicoloured scum bubbled in once
bucolic ponds. "At night," Conn said, "we
could hear this sort of cannon going off"

> *semiology examines the co-opting of*
> *neutral or pastoral concepts such as "climate"*
> *and "ecology." Of course, the word "green"*
> *no longer denotes a colour among other*
> *colours within a neutral spectrum*

a CBC documentary made no attempt to
be impartial when a trembly-voiced narrator
recounted how the couple had to leave their
farm and move to Regina

> *the public broadcaster morphs "news"*
> *into tropes representing a form of nostalgia*
> *for quasi-knowledge free of error and illusion*

4

over 15 million tonnes of carbon dioxide
have been pumped underground. No test
results support claims that CO_2 has migrated
through geological storage

> *young wolves are acting on naïve*
> *ideology proposed by icons like David Suzuki*
> *who organized the wreckage of the "hippies"*
> *into massive concentration camps*

the project covers some 52,000 acres
with a total of 963 active wells, 171 injection
systems. Overall it is anticipated that some 20
Mt of CO_2 will be permanently sequestered

> *Suzuki et al. created a generation*
> *of idealists unable to distinguish carbon*
> *sequestration from their own prison of*
> *enviromancy. Lenin lived in such a zone*
> *of exile in 1898, and Chekhov visited an*
> *activist colony on the Sakhalin Islands*

5

even the Calgary Herald joined the global
media inquisition at the Conn family
conference

> *we must understand how small*
> *individuals, the microbodies of discipline*
> *deploy unexamined tactics (school recycling*
> *programs, litter clean-up projects)*

environmental despotism has
reached the courts which fined Syncrude
more than 3 million for the unintentional
death of ducks on its tailings ponds

> *one can link "justice" and the*
> *transformation of children's bodies into*
> *highly complex systems of manipulation*
> *and conditioning*

6

organizations we considered allies
called for greater government oversight
without citing Industry's comprehensive
seven-page report

> *only precise analysis can excise*
> *the desire of the masses for activism and*
> *reveal public complicity in the refusal to*
> *decipher what environmentalism*
> *(enviromancy) really means*

as an industry we must wrest
the media from its addiction to activist
sensationalism and present our own
isotopes

> *the good news is that now*
> *a majority, possessing an economic*
> *plan can dismantle the social and*
> *cultural hegemony in which activism*
> *operates in our own heads*

PROTOCOLS OF GLOBAL OIL

guidelines from Oil Supermajor
(threatened by poets)

professional advancement

dress your personae in rosy
usury. routinize use of nooses
ban ruinous Mondays

cue up fury. dry your ivory
under cover. conjure a jury
flay day labour in flaming
show trial

suckle nickel. pull bluetooth
execute cuticles. launder toxic
SOX. fix oil tax. exile foes
telex a life. lie to fate

environmental stewardship

cuddle rubies. dandle gradient
berate red bats. lacerate craters
shag an agate. mate tall lattes

repeal base flow. stand down
national flowers. sponsor torpor
police tortoises disguised in
lonesome gorges

luge the Niger. search
debauched birches. confiscate
eldritch. baste foliage
in DDT

respectful workplace

inspect xylem dens
patronize fair trade warlords
acquire microwaveable slaves
detonate failed nations
cremate corn

principles of diversity

start a cartel. halt molten
revolts. root out theatres

sell lactose to acetate cattle
dilate the slate trade. escalate
tidal riots in dead cities

oppose socio-realism. flog
prophets. rope Hopi tropes
usurp tinpot Popes. steer lost
moppets into puppetries

the Americas

dilute the Aleutians
raise your sabre. raid
Canadian nadir. Case-
and-cement Hecate

render cedars unto Caesar
menace coho with spiral-
bound notebooks. hoard
cod. goad badlands

seduce buttes. seal coulees
turn wassailing prairie into
loyal alloy

**action items to preserve
endangered Canadian
hydrocarbons**

Canada must take
ownership of her
homegrown terror

silence species
dissidence

increase speed
and frequency
of manifestos

replace hostile tubers
with shiny tubulars

ban wilderness activity
from access roads, flare
stacks, tailings ponds

subsidize tank farms

raze al-Taxa
training camps

guard bardic
upgraders

cage sabre-
toothed
taiga

SINISTRALE PLC VS THE SIERRA CLUB

a long-chain carbon play

phase 1

**select weapons
and talismans**

choose Ore Robber 400
the Borehole Hero

bond your para-
formaldehydes

load 4" KonShot
Newtonian Cement
xanthan gum

add Cranial Scraper
(Halliburton Lite-
Wate). heat a little
tartrate

calm mad isopachs
mix Pozzolan, Borax
repel off-axis attacks

perforate

flex deltaics. caulk
Grassi Lake. torque
arkose, bottomhole
choke. classic
Verkolak

drop CrossWing Legato
down the long straight
(Sweet Fairway
& Thief)

enter contested
geological regime

joli fou basalt
assaults diamict
shale break at
apical half-angle

Poseidon Tide Rush
in Hades Divide

Shunda truncates
graben burns, red
bed erodes

gored by Nordegg
in siderite corridor

you lose control
of your loess

**Sierra allies with
Greenpeace**

Sierra fires Op-Ed
Sky-Splitter on
the crossbone

Eocene Coincidence
at Omineca Belt
incites Pekiskans

faunal assemblages
bawl pastoral rants
through bullhorns

ERCB demands
your sample

O, Short-Fall
Melancholy

phase 2

retaliate

pump strom

correlate
Dismal Rat
& Carrot Creek
members

panhandle
transient
sandstone

transgressive
sediment from
nameless
paleoslopes

bioturbate
re-direct bit
bait argillite

execute
Lunatic Flip

go horizontal

one ton Stand-
Alone Hit-Stun
on Minotaur Run

**terrorist alliance
enlists celebrities**

Sierra poses
yet another
photo op

displays string
of dead ducks
for Activist Week

stick to littoral
reading

debunk their
Sukunkan *bumf*

declare Tight-Hole
on this leg of play

restructure

disguise Soul-Siphon
in Rising-Night

murmur numbers
down the atrium
plot tomorrow's
gematria

commingle
umbilicals

seismicize

pray Isis presides
over risky sideline

greenwash black ops

validate Level 3
back-reef, Berea
coral area

carbon noids
void crinoid

plumb terminal
moraine

lampshell harem
in Vermilion Hills

Lodestar Strike!

ready, aim, FILE

format Emergency
Planning Zone

drag cursor
over borders
drop native files

rotate thumb
Num Lock
populated fields

scobble variables
bootstrap minor
subgroups. convert
.csv to .xls

comma-separate
Sierran values
deny permissions

liberate data. capture
proprietary scada

chemical scandal
claim amnesia
animate formulae
submit

rubberstamps coo
approved approved
approved

> *Sinistrale PLC receives the Certificate*
> *of World Domination for saving the world*
> *from Energy Depletion*

DOING BUSINESS WITH POETS

Global Guidelines for first-time poetry readings by downtrodden Oil tycoons

1

enemy poets dance
on the stanzas of
mass production

2

orphic forces
stockpile
oracular hats

cadres of losers
aim phrase tasers

hum as they pump
Bedlamite into
children hidden
in Oulippan labs

3

do not fall for
linguists who
would riddle
critics with wit!

last October
they elected
attack dactyls

4
always follow
global protocol

never blindfold
a poet or spirit
one-off in a black
Mariah to Nigeria

South China Sea
without providing
new-hire orientation
dinner at the Westin

5
do not be
a brand hero

never overthrow
a rogue poet
on your own

bribe a fixer
to mollify
syllabic tribes

illegally supplied
with anagram
machines
running
pentameter

a million
rimbauds
a day

6
caught in
stage light

miles from
the nearest
PowerPoint

you can drown
in their ground-
water vowels

7
call for backup

evoke all the orcs
black helicopters
flying monkeys
bookmarked in
your Blackberry

crack their
poetics into
metric feet

process
bellicose
verse

render hostile
lexicon into
honest sonnets

COUNTER-REVOLUTION

royalist defeat

turn Archaeon hairpin bourbons run numbers down
Rubicon One marooned barn owls don brown cowls
new moon draws lewd vowels on the Queen's trianon

pines incite cyanide swamps roar dogma rogue bogs
yodel weird Laramide odes as S-curve hurls Purcells
deny Jurassic reforms grip wheel your knuckles burl

set Homer follow yellow polemics chart moral course
light a right-of-way Rundle opens loins orogeny zone
kyanite arête flirts with Stolberg chert loose republics

whisper promises guileless nephrites romp in borrow-
site clastic action on primal Crown land no one's fault
alums grift drumlins moo rumours of Candu voodoo

stir murderous splurge foothills spill Telluric purists
invoke alluvial stupor Closing Time sovereign dunes
croon Devonian show tunes a carborundum reunion

storming of Fort McMurray

dynamos roam immigrants swarm a new city rents
identity wholesale carousels jump fences state-run
caraganas harangue gypsum caravans GPS frowns

solemn dominos primp travelling wellheads divine
arcane fragonard in bitumen minute cutlines gleam
radium shamen dump Cambrian preamble diatoms

chime smilodons fume lams slump hands 2 and 10
quick shoulder-check Jack-of-Hearts shuck moldic
conocos knock wood tiny Syncrudes claw Lockeian

krill sinkholes wail shells coil in colonial pools drill
bits jive diodes read out today's sweet-verse eskers
rev derricks provoke maverick banalités pangaeans

erupt your 7-league boots putter over spittle caught
in velocity uplift Halliburton lobs a gob of payload
lollipops explode cobbled roads lead to the scaffold

revolutionary justice

you swoon through the lunette sweet Madame
Guillotine keens decimals steam omens bloom
your back aches darkling cycads shrill old Gallic

chansons stocks flush muskets blush cockades
maraud Necker sets dead reckoning pyroclasts
spy hoods wink periwigs defy gravity as credos

seed jolly gallows patrol erotic baldric charters
rot in subaltern waters salty gabelles snack on
suzerain basins threaten tectonic intervention

tea lights rile alien colonies earls twirl reserves
knitting needles purl boreal ore Voltaire flares
harlequins reel unholy carmagnole in Permian

opera purple heliotrope debrief sans-culottes
garotte breccian patriotes Robespierre chutes
lettres de cachet Brazeau loses his boudinage

slip a Louis d'or to the croupiers at the coulees
we say you won this surrender come on down
claim your 6-gun dreamland you are pardoned

6

PANACEA

TENDER CARBON

special to the OilSands Review

editorial by Gertrude Stein

it was a time when in the acres in late
there was a heat-eating wheel that shot a burst of land
dynamic, green and successful. no reason for distress. out of
an eye comes research becomes a seal and matches
and ivy and a suit, all of which is a system
deforestation is a carafe, a spectacle
and nothing strange

Syncrude, if it is not dangerous
then a pleasure. Shell, BP, Sinopec, the Royal Bank
of Scotland, desperate adventure and courage
and a clock. workers flown in from
around the world, a loud clash
and empty wagon
a sign of
extra

wellpads and pipelines are an elegant settlement
a very elegant settlement is more than of consequence. if you suppose
this is in August and even more melodious. if processing
facilities are lily white as lilies, if they exhaust noise
and distance and even dust. if they
dusty will dirt a surface. a
surface will unsurface
if they do this

an upgrader is handily made
of what is necessary to replace any substance
an occasion for a plate. plates and a dinner set
and a petrostate of coloured china. cut
cut in white so lately cause a whole
thing to be a church

humanity's addicts are addicted
to the addiction of oil, consumers and industry, swathes
of boreal forest do so. cut the whole space into twenty-four spaces
a white egg and a coloured pan and a cabbage showing
settlement and constant increase greenwash
the ungreenable. a green acre is so
selfish. there is not only no
excuse. no use there for
no use or uselessness
even worse

an ecosystem is
a splendid address, a really splendid
address, an elegant use of foliage and grace
and a little piece of white cloth and oil
it means no more than
a memory

branded, rebranded
Albian Sands rehabilitated heat-eating
construction sites creating jobs. every time there is
a division there is dividing considering the circumstances
there is no occasion of a reduction. there is no
outage, no outrage, no cause for
reparation

a government exonerates
lower taxes and axioms in the Toxic
Sacrifice Zone. hold the pine, hold the dark
hold in the rush, outsource dreams
Third Party entities make
the bottom

petrochemists, lobbyists
guessing again and golfing again
and the best men, the very best men, decent
do-gooder democracies subsidizing subsidized enterprises
the world's third largest watershed, six barrels water one barrel oil
four tonnes water one barrel oil. four tonnes earth
one barrel oil make a little white
no and not with pit
pit on in within

for engineering
and geology students beyond petroleum there are
free wine and canapes, rustic treats. duck livers please
be the beef. please beef, please be carved clear
the result, the pure result is juice and size
and baking and exhibition and
nonchalance and sacrifice
and volume

tars and reserves
have a plan, a hearty plan, a plan
that has excess and that break is the one
that shows filling. any neglect of oil revenue is neglect
any neglect of many particles to a cracking
any neglect of this makes around it
what is lead in colour

water, astonishing and difficult
altogether makes the lamp, the cake
the walleye fish enthusiastically hurting
a clouded yellow bud and saucer. loonies feed
off tales told at the tail end
of the tailings

failed Copenhagen talks do cause
seepage. the indigenous dignitaries indignantly
re-sign treaty rights in igneous ink. there is no authority
for the abuse of cheese. climate summits jam
everyone's downstream. it means no
more than memory

breach of impoundment
a little lunch. boil solvent, melt bitumen. steep
arsenic, cyanide, naphthenic acids. this is no dark
custom. more is almost enough and just so much more is there
plenty of reason for making an exchange. more
is almost enough. pond surplus pop
bond yield

what is the wind, what is it
what is the current that makes machinery
that makes it crackle through unlined dykes. what
is this current, where is the serene length
of a polycyclic aromatic, it is there
and a dark place is not the
frightful release of an
umbrella

where is the serene length, it is there
and a dark place is not a dark place, groundwater
that is grounded is a dark grey, a very dark
grey, a quite grey is monstrous because
there is no red in it. is that not
an argument for any
use of it

removing the overburden opens
the new a new useable crude. cool nuclear
reactors, microbial bloomings, G8 careers and
vocations, mutated fish alarms
any little thing
is water

a plain hill, an unfair trade barrier
a failed Copenhagen talk makes no sunshine. the place
was replaced. this does not mean the same as disappearing
a climate, a single climate, all the time there is a single
climate. a lake a single lake which is a pond
a little leaf upon a scene, an ocean any
where there, a bland and likely in
the stream, a recollection
green land. it means
no more memory

the care
with which the rain is wrong
and the green is wrong and the white is wrong. the care
with which there is incredible justice and likeness
all this makes a magnificent
asparagus and also
a fountain

ADVANCES IN UNCONVENTIONAL ONEIROLOGY

at 25 barrels per capita
(60 barrels Alberta)
Canadians are the world's
heaviest dream users

my subconscious contains
a semantic core encased
in mundane sand, sulphur
salt water

heat, pressure, decay
eventually compress
past and present into
a tarry ooze

early oneirologists ran
small diameter pipes
through my limbic
system

flared off random
thought mutations
until my amygdala
blew out on Seepage
Lake

for weeks, phantasms
and psychoses clogged
the Old Man River
terrorizing Lethbridge

finally in '55 the great
Conrad Schlumberger
analyzed a lump of my
reverie and just knew

dimethyltriptamine
could increase dream
production 60%

Imperial Oil approved
gravimetric testing on
my hippocampus

cholinergic ponto-genicul-
occipital waves stimulated
my cortical structures

technicians injected
nitroglycerine into my
parietal lobe

shot-point vibrations
released dissociated
imagination from
sensory traps

REM converters allowed
thousands of metres of
uncaptured by-products
to push up the standpipe

rendering a whole new
source of my dreams
(whimsy, hypnagogia)
safe for your factory
your car, your furnace

HEAVY OIL: A LOVER'S DISCOURSE

the unknowable

efforts of the amorous subject to understand and define
the loved being "in itself," by some standard of character type,
psychological or neurotic personality, independent of the particular
data of the amorous relation

1. i believe i know the other better than anyone and
    triumphantly assert my knowledge to the other (we
    need a gravel road out to this value – there will be a
    building here. make road larger, less than 40 m for
    road top, 10 cm rig access)

2. of everyone I had known, wo6 was certainly the most
    impenetrable. (process road where? road for chemical
    off-loading?) who is the other? i wear myself out, i
    shall never know

3. it is not true that the more you love, the better you
    understand. (is this curve designed for the speed limit?
    compared to?) i am often seized with that exaltation
    of loving *someone* unknown, someone who will remain
    so forever

to love love

annulation / annulment

explosion of language during which the subject manages to
annul the loved object under the volume of love itself: by a
specifically amorous perversion, it is love the subject loves
not the object

1.   w06 is quite insipid; she is the paltry character of a
        tormented flamboyant drama staged by the subject

2.   any wellpad could be placed in the centre of the stage
        adored, idolized, taken to task, covered with discourse
        it is my desire i desire

agony

angoisse / agony

the amorous subject, according to one contingency or another
feels swept away by the fear of a danger, an injury, an abandonment
a revulsion – a sentiment he expresses under the name of *anxiety*

1.   tonight i came back to wo6 alone. the anxieties are
already here like the poison already prepared. (we cannot
build if there is no crossing agreement. please confirm
elevation is acceptable for piperack crossing.)

2.   the silence of the ash silos and slop tanks is echoing
nothing friendly that might warm. anxiety mounts
feeling the cold of hemlock rising in the very area
reserved for the pigging skid

3.   it is the fear of a mourning that has already occurred
at the first ramp, the very origin of love, where i was
first ravished. the notion of suicide occurs to me

the absent one

absence / absence

any episode of language which stages the absence of the loved
object – whatever its cause and its duration – and which tends to
transform this absence into an ordeal of abandonment

1.   many lieder songs and mélodies about site-specific
               timber-salvaging plans. also included here topsoil/
               subsoil-stripping miraculously feminized

2.   sometimes i have no difficulty enduring absence
               topsoil must be stockpiled on firm ground. then
               i am "normal." i fall in with the way everyone
               moves datum. i behave as a well-weaned subject
               grade sloping *down* towards NE

i am engulfed

s'abimer / to be engulfed

outburst of annihilation which affects the amorous subject
in despair or fulfillment

1.   either woe or well-being, sometimes i have a craving
         to be engulfed. this morning the weather is mild
         overcast. (what do we do for water run-off control
         during construction?)

2.   another day in the rain waiting for the boat at the lake
         the same burst of annihilation sweeps through me
         (water will be trapped here. need culvert? please
         verify calculations/sizing)

3.   this is how it happens sometimes, misery or joy
         engulfs me. i fall, i flow, i melt. (pond capacity
         appears too small. need means of pumping into
         process road. the water in this pool will have to be
         tested before it is released into the environment.)

4.   engulfment is a moment of hypnosis. we die
         together from loving each other: an open death
         (secondary containment liner and leak detection
         system not required at this site)

the last leaf

magie / magic

whether he seeks to prove his love, or to discover if the other
loves him, the amorous subject has no system of sure signs
at his disposal

1.   here and there, on the trees, some leaves remain and i
            contemplate 1,500 mm fill to consolidate the muskeg
            prior to placement of common fill material one (1)
            layer of high-strength woven geotextile shall be
            installed over the muskeg

2.   when the wind plays with the leaf, i tremble in every
            limb. (how is emulsion viscosity calculated? this looks
            too low.) and if 3 different specifications for microns
            should fall, alas, my hope falls

the uncertainty of signs

signes / signs

magic consultations, secret rites, and votive actions are not
absent from the amorous subject's life, whatever culture
he belongs to

1.   i look for signs, but of what? arrows the wrong
       direction. drawn date cannot be August 25 if Rev A
       was issued April 13; what is the object of my
       reading? is it: am i loved (am i loved no longer
       am I still loved)?

2.   according to a method which combines paleography
       and manticism there are no existing boreholes at the
       site. i remain suspended on this question, whose
       answer i tirelessly seek in the other's face: *why does*
       this drawing not match earlier ones?

3.   as in any manticism, the construction contractor shall
       verify the existing conditions prior to construction

4.   signs are not proofs since anyone can produce false
       ambiguous signs. where conflict exists between
       construction drawings and actual site conditions
       i shall receive every word from my other as a sign
       of truth; and when i speak, i shall not doubt that
       he, too, receives what i say as the truth

MOTIVATIONAL QUOTATIONS

from **wisdominthesands.com**

despite your best intentions
horizontal multi-stage frac projects
tend to go exponential

conceptual art is an unintentional
consequence of low oil prices

when discussing dirty oil always
jump in with the chicken and egg
analogy. substitute apples and
oranges when necessary

wholeness consists of extraction
upgrading, coal gasification and
electricity generation

it is sufficient to demonstrate
the existence of a carbonate pilot

essentially you can only fertilize
microbes already existing in the
reservoir

you are the only one who can
control heavy oil viscosity

NOTES

All of the poems in this project are derived from texts generated in a multinational oil company. I spliced items such as wellbooks, mudlogs, geological prognoses, and meeting notes with a variety of found material, including histories and critical theoretical works, as well as travel, real estate, and home decor magazines – basically anything that crossed my path.

Partial list of sources:

Allen, Thomas O., and Alan P. Roberts. *Production Operations: Well Completions, Workover and Stimulation.* 2 vols. Tulsa: Oil & Gas Consultants International, 1982.

Barthes, Roland. *A Lover's Discourse.* NY: Hill & Wang, 2010.

Berger, Thomas R. *Northern Frontier, Northern Homeland: The Report of the Mackenzie Valley Pipeline Inquiry.* 2 vols. Ottawa: Supply and Services Canada, 1977.

Blume, Mary. *Côte d'Azur: Inventing the French Riviera.* NY: Thames and Hudson, 1992.

Foucault, Michel. *Power/Knowledge: Selected Interviews and Other Writings 1972–1977.* NY: Pantheon, 1980.

Gardner, Laurence. *The Shadow of Solomon: The Lost Secret of the Freemasons Revealed.* San Francisco: Weiser, 2007.

Heavy Oil & Oilsands Guidebook. Spec. issue of *The Oilsands Review,* 2012.

James, Henry. *Transatlantic Sketches.* Boston: Houghton, Mifflin & Co., 1875.

Jung, Carl. *Man and His Symbols.* NY: Dell, 1979.

Lovecraft, H.P. *The Case of Charles Dexter Ward.* NY: Ballantine, 1976.

Nelson, Samuel J. *The Face of Time: The Geological History of Western Canada*. Calgary: Alberta Society of Petroleum Geologists, 1970.

Schama, Simon. *Citizens: A Chronicle of the French Revolution*. NY: Alfred A. Knopf, 1989.

Stein, Gertrude. *Look at Me Now and Here I Am: Writings and Lectures 1909–45*. Ed. Patricia Meyerowitz. NY: Penguin, 1967.

Tosches, Nick. *Where Dead Voices Gather*. Boston: Little Brown & Co., 2001.

ACKNOWLEDGEMENTS

First of all, to Fred Van Driel for bad puns, pizza, and road trips, especially the one to Inuvik/Tuk, which influenced this work so much.

For his generous support of this project, a big thank-you to Tom Wayman.

I would also like to thank the editors of *Arc, CV2, dANDelion, filling Station, Other Voices, PRISM international,* and *West Coast Line* for publishing earlier versions of some of these poems. Especially Anita Lahey, Jordan Abel, and Paul Zits for such a warm welcome to the publishing world.

And of course, thanks to everyone at the University of Calgary: Christian Bök, who rewired a few neurons; Aritha van Herk, who threatened me with farm implements; and my fellow travellers, who have taught me so much.

Lesley Battler's work has been published in *Alberta Views, Arc, Contemporary Verse 2, dANDelion, filling Station, Matrix, Other Voices, PRISM international,* and *West Coast Line.* She won the *PRISM international* Earle Birney Award (2012), and the University of Calgary Poem of the Season Award (2009) for a poem that became part of *Endangered Hydrocarbons.* Battler received an MA in English from Concordia University, and currently lives in Calgary, where she works in the petrochemical industry.

COLOPHON

Manufactured as the First Edition
of *Endangered Hydrocarbons* in the
Spring of 2015 by BookThug

Distributed in Canada by the
Literary Press Group www.lpg.ca

Distributed in the US by
Small Press Distribution www.spdbooks.org

Shop online at www.bookthug.ca

BOOK
PRODUCTION
WAR ECONOMY
STANDARD

Edited for the press by Phil Hall
Copy edited by Ruth Zichter
Type + design by Jay MillAr